CHILDREN of the MIDNIGHT SUN
Young Native Voices of Alaska

Profiles by
Tricia Brown

Photographs by
Roy Corral

Alaska Northwest Books™
Anchorage • Seattle • Portland

For Lillian Powers Stinson, my inspiration, and Kierra Jordan Morris, my delight.

—T. B.

To Kim, Hannah, and Ben for teaching me the meaning of family.

—R. C.

Acknowledgments

For your giving spirits, direction, and kindness, we thank:
Frank and Rosa Alby, Dan and Dora Ausdahl, the Reverend Martin Ausdahl,
Aquilina Bourdukofsky, Neil and Geraldine Charlie, the Reverend Steven Epchook,
Wayne and Toni Hewson, Jones and Lani Hotch, Dr. Michael Krauss of the Alaska Native
Language Center at the University of Alaska Fairbanks, Larry Merculieff, Ben and
Bonnie Nageak, Carl and Andrea Thompson, and Pat and Christine Tolson.

In memory of Mr. and Mrs. Sylvester Peele of Hydaburg, who shared generously in every way.

*A portion of the author's proceeds will benefit the
Alaska Native Heritage Center in Anchorage, a place for gathering, learning, and renewal.
For more information on the nonprofit center, or to make a donation, contact:
Alaska Native Heritage Center, 2525 Cordova Street, Suite 425, Anchorage, Alaska 99503.
Call (907) 263-5170 or fax (907) 263-5575.*

Photos. *Title page:* Yup'ik girls dance at Alaska Federation of Natives, Anchorage.
Page 2: Lower Kalskag boys use a boat motor cover as a sled.
Page 5: Iñupiat boy and drummers. *Back of book:* Katiana Bourdukofsky and Heidi Merculieff,
Aleut girls from St. Paul Island, rest among the wildflowers.

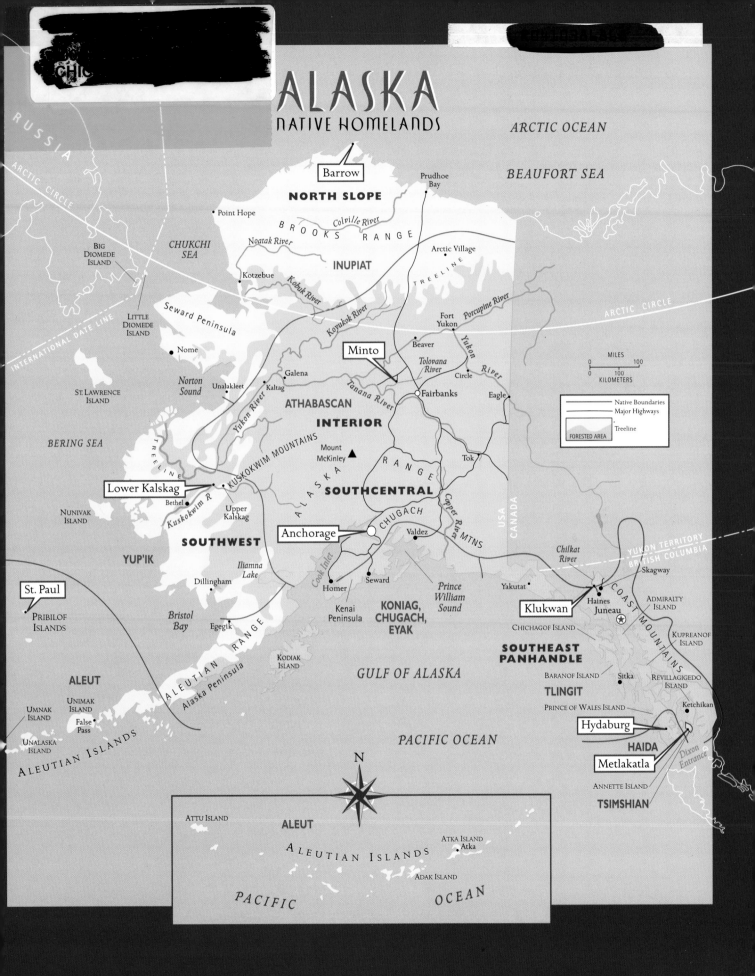

Contents

Foreword by Larry Merculieff 6
Introduction: Yesterday and Today 8

12

16

1

I Live at the Top of the World 12
Robert Nageak, Iñupiat

2

In the Footsteps of My Grandfather 16
John Charlie, Athabascan

20

24

3

I'm a Daughter of the Pribilof Islands 20
Katiana Bourdukofsky, Aleut

4

The Ocean Feeds Our Family 24
Selina Tolson, Haida

28

32

5

Russian Christmas on the Kuskokwim River 28
Andrea Hoelscher, Yup'ik

6

I'm Happy To Be an Island Boy 32
Danny Hewson, Tsimshian

36

40

7

My Journey to Tlingit Manhood 36
Josh Hotch, Tlingit

8

Bright Lights and My Big Village 40
Tauni Thompson, Aleut-Caucasian

Glossary 44
Recommended Reading 47

Foreword

Frost patterns coat the windows of Andrea Hoelscher's church.

In my thirty-some years of working with and for Alaska Native peoples, I have had the privilege of visiting more than sixty Native villages throughout Alaska. Like all those of my generation, I have witnessed incredible changes in our cultures and lifestyles over this period. Many of those changes have been brought about by the introduction of television, improved communications and transportation systems, and, of course, the computer and the Internet. Modern technologies bring new challenges and opportunities to all Alaska Natives, but perhaps none greater than those presented to the generations born in the 1980s and 1990s.

Today's up-and-coming generations will have to deal with a world much more compressed and interconnected than ever experienced by anyone to this point in time. Their primary challenge may be to retain and enhance the wisdom of their cultures as our communities become less and less isolated and as the lure of the material world intensifies. Their primary opportunity may be to participate in what the Wisdomkeepers call the time of the Whirling Rainbow, a time of reconnection of peoples of the four sacred colors—red, white, black, and yellow—which is to manifest in this lifetime.

6

Hopefully the new generations of Alaska Natives will listen to the voices of experience and wisdom; however, the elders say that children mirror the walk of adults. If the adults wish for the young to listen to what we have to say about our lessons in life, we must show the way by the manner in which we listen and show respect for all others, including the Children of the Midnight Sun. This book gives everyone another avenue for listening to what our children are saying.

Tricia Brown brings keen perception to what she chooses to document in this book about what our children are saying and the challenges they face. Tricia came to Alaska in 1978, and for nearly twenty years she has put her heart and mind into many stories involving Alaska Natives, as a writer and editor for the *Fairbanks Daily News-Miner*, the *Anchorage Daily News*, *Alaska* magazine, and other publications. She has received numerous awards for her writing, editing, and photography. In *Children of the Midnight Sun*, Tricia skillfully tells the story of our young people during a period of tremendous change.

I can think of no more beautiful complement to Tricia Brown's work than the sensitive and poignant photography of Roy Corral, a lecturer, teacher, and photographer. Roy Corral's work has appeared in more than thirty publications, including *National Geographic, Alaska Geographic*, the *Los Angeles Times*, and *Sports Illustrated for Kids*. He is also the recipient of numerous photographic awards. Roy has added depth to his understanding of Alaska Native peoples and the issues we face in his work counseling Native students and directing public service job placement for forty-three Doyon Corporation villages in Interior Alaska, as a subregional director for the Tanana Chiefs Conference, and as a Johnson O'Malley and adult education program director for the Fairbanks Native Association.

Together, in *Children of the Midnight Sun*, Tricia Brown and Roy Corral weave a story that contains messages for everyone, young and old alike. The prophecies as told by the Wisdomkeepers predicted this time of the Whirling Rainbow, when those of the Sacred White Color will help those of the Sacred Red Color because, although their outer garment is white, inside they are red. Roy and Tricia, I believe, are part of the fulfillment of those prophecies.

—Larry Merculieff
Aleut

Introduction
Yesterday and Today

An Iñupiat girl dances at the Alaska Federation of Natives convention in Anchorage.

One spring day, not long ago, a relentless storm chewed away at a bluff overlooking the Arctic Ocean at Point Barrow, the northernmost tip of land in America. As wind and pounding rain carried away chunks of soil, the ancient grave of a little girl was exposed. She was curled into a ball and clothed in a feather parka made of bird skins. The girl had been covered with a baleen sled in the cellar of a sod home that had later caved in, and there she'd rested for perhaps 8,000 years. The bluff held other treasure, too—hand-carved wooden bowls, trade beads, a bear-skin mukluk, a mitten made from polar bear hide. Some things were a few hundred years old; others were ancient.

Scientists turned to Barrow's Native elders for help in identifying the artifacts. Incredibly, even though a few objects had been buried for thousands of years, some elders recognized them. Their parents and grandparents had talked about or used similar tools or clothing. Some elders even remembered growing up in sod homes something like the girl's. That's how little certain ways of the Iñupiat Eskimo people had changed. Until now.

Today, a girl growing up in Barrow can ride to the store on a snowmachine, on a four-wheeler, or in a car, and look over the fresh fruit and vegetables as her parents pick up pizza and videos. Or dinner might instead be boiled bowhead whale meat, a portion of her family's share from the last whaling season. She may snack on Doritos and M&M's or on slices of frozen whale blubber, called muktuk. On Saturday, she can watch cartoons carried via satellite or she might shoot hoops at the gym.

Life for today's Alaska Native children is a meld of cultures, accepted Western ways among treasured Native ways, a mingling of ancient and modern. Only in the last twenty-five years has satellite television brought the values of modern America into their homes. Advertisers persuade young people to buy the latest clothes, toys, and video games. Actors portray a "me first" way of thinking. And yet Native elders are teaching just the opposite. They remind the children about the importance of community, responsibility to their people, sharing, and survival—lessons that have been passed along since before memory.

The first Alaskans, researchers say, were among those who migrated to North America from Asia across the Bering Land Bridge, a narrow stretch of land that's now underwater. On a journey that began at least a hundred centuries ago, some of the travelers moved on to other places in North, Central, and even South America. Over time, Alaska was populated by three major groups: Eskimos, Indians, and Aleuts.

When the first European explorer, Vitus Bering, landed in 1741, each of the largest Native groups already had well-defined territorial boundaries, with little intermarriage but much trade. The treeless, wind-swept Arctic belonged to the Iñupiat Eskimos; the southwestern coastal areas and wetlands were home to the Yup'ik Eskimos; every major island in the Aleutians was inhabited by expert navigators, the Aleuts; the nomadic Athabascan Indians claimed the vast Interior and some of Southcentral Alaska; and the Tlingit Indians dominated the rain forest of Southeast.

In the 250 years since first contact, waves of outsiders have descended on Alaska, from the earliest Europeans, who came to get rich on the fur trade, to missionaries, miners, and the military who followed. The Alaska Highway, built during World War II as a wartime supply line, connected Alaska with the Lower 48 states and created even easier access for travelers and settlers. Today, Alaska's non-Native population easily outnumbers Native residents.

Tauni Thompson studies a fast-food menu at Anchorage's Fifth Avenue Mall.

How has all this affected the Eskimos, Indians, and Aleuts? In some ways, few Natives would go back to the old days. They appreciate the conveniences brought by the outsiders, including rifles, boat motors, grocery stores, airplanes, and telephones. But in the beginning, back in the late 1700s, contact with Europeans meant death for thousands from disease, starvation, and war with foreigners. Resources of fish and fur-bearing animals were diminished. New arrivals forced their rule and customs on the indigenous people.

Even those who wished to help the Alaska Natives seem to have brought mixed blessings. Early Russian Orthodox churchman Father Ioann Veniaminov learned the Aleut and Tlingit languages and created written alphabets so he could translate the Bible. Today, most Aleuts are Orthodox Christians, and little of pre-contact Aleut culture remains. In 1877, Sheldon Jackson, a Presbyterian minister, was directed by the U.S. government to establish schools in Alaska. To stretch his small budget, he divided the territory among various Christian denominations for schools and other missionary work. Today, many are critical of Jackson's plan, especially Alaska Natives who were treated harshly if they spoke their own language in school. Others readily adopted a new language and religion. For decades, teachers and church leaders discouraged many Native cultural traditions, such as dancing and singing, labeling them as either demonic or simply strange and unacceptable.

The grandparents of today's Alaska Native children remember those days. As young adults, they continued to fish and hunt to feed their families, but to dance, or sing, or speak in their Native tongue? That was taboo. So was teaching those things to their own children, and an entire generation grew up without a complete cultural education.

As the twentieth century began to wind down, however, a cultural rebirth began, quietly and surely, in small pockets that grew. Young Native leaders, hungry for traditional knowledge, looked to their elders for direction. Artisans asked older craftspeople to teach them how to weave, carve, or sew skins. Where dances and songs were absent, the young people experimented. Arts associations and dance groups were formed. The elders' stories from their lifetimes and earlier were recorded. Culture camps sprang up. And, in the midst of this rebirth, another generation came on the scene with eager, teachable minds.

Today, in Juneau, a biannual cultural reunion called Celebration attracts hundreds of Southeast Natives. In Fairbanks, Natives converge annually for the Festival of Native Arts and the World Eskimo-Indian Olympics. Anchorage hosts the annual meeting of the Alaska Federation of Natives, organized to discuss issues affecting Natives statewide and to present a united voice in political matters.

The old ones still have much to share with their descendants . . . if they will watch and listen. Television, telephones, CDs, sports, and computers compete with what little time the elders have left to teach.

Are the children listening? When they are older, will they remember a childhood accompanied by Barbie, the X-Men, the Internet, Burger King, and the Disney Channel? Or are Alaska Native families successfully mingling the ancient ways with the Cyber Age?

For some answers, photographer Roy Corral and I traveled throughout Alaska visiting a generation of Native children who will become adults in the twenty-first century. We met boys and girls, with help from teachers, village leaders, tribal chiefs, heritage camp activists, parents, and elders.

Life is indeed a complicated balancing act for today's Native children, we found, but they are gifted with good balance. You'll meet eight of them in the following profiles. Asked about their favorite foods, the kids listed tacos and french fries right along with moosehead soup and muktuk. They play computer games and basketball as well as compete in the two-foot kick, an Eskimo game of old. They can tell us about today's news or a story from long, long ago.

Back in Barrow, where the grave of the ancient child was discovered, village elders allowed limited scientific study before the girl was returned to the earth. Plans were made for a Christian burial in the town cemetery. Teachers used this opportunity for their students to learn more about the ancients, and about the importance of cultural survival, then and now. Third-graders held "pretend" archeological digs in the classroom, talked about the artifacts from the bluff, and imagined what life was like back then. They drew pictures and wrote letters to the little girl. And on the day the girl was laid to rest again, children came to say good-bye to an ancestor. This time her grave had a marker, and on it was the Eskimo name given to her by these children. *Agnaiyaaq*, it read. Young Girl.

A young dancer waits to go on stage at the Alaska Federation of Natives convention in Anchorage.

1

I Live at the Top of the World

Robert Nageak

Robert Nageak is snacking on Doritos when his mother pulls out a plastic bag of *maktaq*, the layer of skin and blubber from a bowhead whale. With her kitchen *ulu*, the U-shaped Eskimo "women's knife," she slices off pieces of the raw, frozen treat. Quickly the Doritos are forgotten.

Frozen, salted, or boiled, *maktaq* is a favorite for the Nageak kids—Robert, Eva, and Perry—and their parents, Ben and Bonnie. The whale meat beneath the *maktaq* is equally delicious, says Bonnie, and the family especially likes it fried with onions. Other nights, she may prepare caribou, fish, or seal. Or maybe hamburgers.

The Nageaks are from Barrow, America's northernmost city, where most of the 4,300 residents are Iñupiat Eskimo. It's a windswept community of log and frame buildings on a treeless landscape. No roads lead here; everybody flies in or out.

Robert, twelve, has covered the area by foot, all-terrain vehicle, and snowmachine. His favorite place is along Avuk Creek, about twenty minutes out of town, where he can watch the caribou.

"It's real pretty," Robert says. "The calves roam around the creek, and the bulls . . . man! When you see the bulls, their antlers are huge—they're like four feet across."

Snow covers Barrow from September to May, and kids slide down windblown drifts or play football if it's not too cold. There's usually a basketball game at the school gym. The average high in February is fourteen degrees below zero and, with wind chill, temperatures can reach eighty below. In winter, the

◄ *In his uncle's whaling boat, Robert wears his camouflage white hunting parka.* ▲ *Robert (left) and Perry cut off some bite-size pieces of* maktaq *for an afternoon snack. Robert uses his sharp hunting knife, while Perry chooses an* ulu.

13

Robert and Eva drive around town on an all-terrain vehicle, more commonly called a four-wheeler. Standing water is everywhere when spring breakup comes to Barrow.

sun goes down in November and doesn't return for months, but the aurora borealis occasionally colors the sky. Summer days can reach the high forties, and the Midnight Sun shines for months on end.

Despite the harsh climate, people have lived here for more than 10,000 years. Traditionally, Iñupiats built semi-underground homes that were supported with whale ribs and driftwood. Wood-frame houses came with the Yankee whalers in the late 1800s.

"In Iñupiaq, *iglu* means 'house,'" Robert says. "So we live in an *iglu*." The domed ice houses most people think of as *iglus* were actually just temporary shelters, he says. Robert's *"iglu"* is a cozy, three-bedroom home that rests on pilings, like most of the houses here.

"If they put the houses flat on the ground, they'd sink in the mud," he explains. Below the ground-cover roots, the soil is permanently frozen as far as 2,000 feet down. The weight of a regular foundation would cause the permafrost to melt and result in shifting.

Just down Robert's street, car-size chunks of ice still crowd the Arctic Ocean beach in late May. It snowed ten inches recently, then melted. The Nageaks walk on boards across the mud to their house. Boots stay in the Arctic entry, an enclosed porch, along with *atigis*, or parkas.

"This is a hunting parka," Robert says as he pulls a white parka over his head. It has no buttons or zippers, just his hunting knife attached at one side. The hood and cuffs are trimmed with thick fur. "There are dress parkas, for dressing up real nice and going to dances, and there's this kind of parka— it blends in with the snow, so you're protected or hidden from any animals."

In the Far North, polar bears roam the coast for seals, caribou nibble on lichens, arctic foxes hunt for lemmings, wolves feed on baby caribou, and thousands of waterfowl nest in the wetlands.

Barrow's children are learning the Iñupiaq names of animals from village elders, their parents, and in a school elective that covers everything from language to skin sewing and storytelling.

"*Nagluk* means 'goose,' and *ivuk* is 'walrus,'" Robert demonstrates. "*Aġviq* is 'bowhead whale,' *igniq* is 'fire,' and *ugruk* is 'bearded seal.'" In a pause, Eva says, "And *nanuq* means 'polar bear.'"

In and out of class, the children have handled the stone lamps their ancestors used for heat and light. They've learned how baleen from bowhead whales was used for making utensils, lightweight sleds, and baskets.

Robert and his brother, Perry, have also learned by watching when they join the men on hunting trips. Robert prefers to scout around on land, hunting for caribou and ducks. He brags about his brother's hunting skill on ice and water.

Demonstrating his high-kicking ability, Robert (right) gets his friend to hold up one end of an Eskimo yo-yo, made of two fur-covered balls connected by a string.

Even traditional games are related to hunting—springing from exercises in strength, agility, and courage. Each Christmas, locals compete in games such as the one- and two-foot kick, the ear pull, and the knuckle hop.

One year, Robert won the two-foot kick by kicking a suspended ball with both feet and then landing on both feet without falling. "That was four feet, ten inches," Robert says, holding a picture of himself in action. "I was four feet, eight inches tall."

Suddenly, Benjamin Nageak bursts in loudly, smiling and alert even though he hasn't slept in more than twenty-four hours. The Akootchook Whaling Crew landed a spring bowhead whale last night, so today the Akootchook flag will fly above the captain's house, signaling that shares of the whale are available.

The practice of whaling and the beliefs surrounding it—respect for the animal, sharing the kill, and celebrating a whale's gift of itself—are central to the Iñupiats. They believe that every creature has a spirit that must be honored and thanked when it offers itself to sustain the people.

Unlike their ancestors, the Nageaks also live in a cash economy. Ben and Bonnie both have jobs. If they want to escape to Hawaii during the bitter cold, they do. If the village is unable to capture its quota of whales, they can go to the grocery store.

In June, Barrow will gather for *Nalukataq*, the whale-catch festival. At the beach, there'll be feasting, dancing, and another ancient game that Robert never misses: the blanket toss. The Iñupiats do it now as they've done for centuries.

During his turn, Robert will climb onto a large, sealskin blanket. Around it, his family and friends will be holding rope handles and chanting as they gently lift the blanket and Robert in a light bounce. Then, with one big heave, up he'll go, ten to fifteen feet into the air, holding his breath and kicking to stay upright—just as his grandfathers did when they were boys, and their grandfathers did before them.

"I'm not afraid of falling," Robert says, grinning. "I do it every year."

2

In the Footsteps of My Grandfather

John Charlie ATHABASCAN

John Charlie, an Athabascan Indian boy from Minto, is sprawled across the couch in a cabin where he lives with his grandparents. He just got off a plane, back from a cross-country ski meet in Kaltag, 250 air miles away. Like other athletes in small, rural Alaskan schools, he travels for most sports competitions in small planes, not team buses. The aircraft connect villages across conference areas the size of some states.

At thirteen, John dresses like kids anywhere—jeans, T-shirt, and athletic shoes—except his winter wear includes a parka and beaverskin hat and mitts. And in his closet are garments for potlatch dances or other special events.

"My dance clothes are made of moosehide and beads," John says. "Indian vest, slippers, headband, gloves, and necklace."

John's hometown of Minto lies on a bluff overlooking the Tolovana River in the Interior. About 250 Athabascan residents hold a commanding view of Minto Flats, a prime spot for fall duck hunters.

"When you're in a plane or up on a mountain, you can see lots of lakes and islands," John says, describing the flats. "The lakes are almost all connected. People from Minto, we know our way around them."

Outside, a dozen sled dogs, his cousin's team, are staked out in the snowy birch trees. Dog teams once outnumbered snowmachines in Athabascan villages, but now winter travel on the traplines and the rivers—the highways for Interior Alaska villages—is mostly by snow-go, or snowmachine.

Minto is centered in the traditional Athabascan area, so far inland that the people were virtually unaffected by the arrival of Russian fur traders and settlers two centuries ago. But this isn't the first Minto. In about 1915, Episcopal churchmen asked area Natives, who were traditionally a nomadic people, to come together so their children could be educated. At what is now called Old Minto, about ten children were taught by an Episcopal missionary.

John's grandfather, Neil Charlie, remembers how that teacher gave the people Western names by using the first name of a father as the last name for a child. So the son of a man named John was Titus

◄ *A wet greeting from a sled dog.* ▲ *John and his grandfather, Neil Charlie. John's vest, beaver-trimmed gloves, and headband are beaded moosehide. He holds a* ganhok, *used to control sound during potlatch dances.*

Minto is surrounded by plenty of snowy trails, where John loves to cross-country ski. Basketball is another popular sport among Minto kids.

John, and his son was Wilson Titus. John's grandfather was renamed by other missionaries who changed his birth name of "Neah" to Neil. His last name came from his uncle, Chief Charlie, who helped care for him.

Twenty-two miles away by the winter trail, the remains of Old Minto decay along the Yukon River, since the villagers, weary of dealing with spring flooding and swampy land, relocated to the new Minto in the late 1960s.

Athabascans once claimed all of Interior Alaska and part of Southcentral, the broadest region of any Native group, with the most extreme temperature swings—ranging from summer days in the eighties to periods in winter of forty to fifty below zero. Along their territorial borders, Athabascans adopted some of their neighbors' ways, such as using Eskimo-style *ulus* and Tlingit-style bentwood boxes.

When John's grandfather was born in 1919, the

Minto people remained fairly untouched, even by gold miners who'd come to the Interior. Fairbanks was a bustling city, but it was several days' walk away. The people spoke their Native language. They hunted big game and birds, and fished for salmon, pike, whitefish, and grayling. They trapped muskrats, beavers, and rabbits for food and fur, and collected berries and eggs. The people viewed the animals as fellow creatures with spirits worthy of respect. The *deyenenh*, or medicine man, was the liaison between the physical and spiritual worlds of men and animals.

Much has changed in one lifetime. The life John leads bears little resemblance to his grandfather's boyhood. Neil Charlie is now among the Minto elders calling for a return to the old ways, but with a spiritual life based on biblical teachings. He and his wife, Geraldine, speak against drugs, alcohol, divorce, and other harmful influences within their community.

"The first thing we'd like is for young people to get guidance from God," Neil Charlie says, "and to get more of their Native ways back, like the language and Native songs. Also, listen to good advice about how to direct their lives in a better way. These are a strong part of the Native ways."

Neil Charlie calls it "Native school," lessons you can't find in a book and what he's been teaching Minto kids at culture camp.

From his grandfather, John has learned how to set a rabbit snare, how to trap *dzen*, or muskrat, how to build an emergency shelter, and where to look for moose. Even though he has yet to kill his first moose, he's ready.

In the old days, a first moose, or *denèegee*, may have been cause for a potlatch. Potlatches—including feasting, dances, speeches, and singing—remain an essential tradition. With a sharing theme similar to

Villagers along Alaska's great rivers count on salmon runs to help feed them year-round. The fish are split and hung to dry on outdoor racks. Lower quality fish are used for dog food.

the potlatches of the Southeast Alaska Indians, Athabascan potlatches honor important events, such as the coming of spring, a holiday, or a memorial to honor the dead. Unlike the Tlingits, Athabascans don't have strict clan customs surrounding the potlatch.

At his chair by the window, John's grandfather is whittling a *ganhok*, or dance stick, which is used to change the volume during dances.

"Whenever the people go too quiet, the leader lifts up the stick to make it louder," John explains. "If it's too loud, he brings the stick down."

John is an enthusiastic dancer at every potlatch. His moosehide headband features a beaded eagle, not because of any clan affiliation, but because he liked the design. While his ancestors decorated their clothing with porcupine quills, *ch'etth'ena'* (dentalium), and decorative seeds, after contact with Westerners in the 1800s they also used commercially produced beads, floral patterns, and brightly colored yarn tassels.

"My auntie and my grandma do all the beading," John says. "I'm learning from my Grandma Susie. It kinda gets frustrating after awhile."

Along with dancing at potlatches, John looks forward to the great Indian food, especially his favorite, moosehead soup.

"They soft-boil moose," John says, "and make it into soup and stuff. We eat porcupine, beaver, chicken, ducks, muskrats, and pike eggs."

Asked what lessons he will one day pass along to his own children, John pauses thoughtfully before he answers: "I mostly want to teach my children how to hunt moose and ducks and how to survive in the wilderness.

"My grandpa is my best teacher."

3

I'm a Daughter of the Pribilof Islands

Katiana Bourdukofsky

ALEUT

Ten-year-old Katiana Bourdukofsky and her friend Samantha Zacharof may have an audience of just two people, but they are enthusiastic performers.

"This is the sea lion dance," announces Katiana. "In Aleut dances, we act out a story when we're dancing."

Where Katiana lives, the meat and fur of seals and sea lions are important resources. The dance is about an Aleut hunter. At the end, her arm swings down in a sweeping motion. "See?" she says. "We're bringing down the club."

Katiana is among the 739 people who live on St. Paul Island in a village with the same name. St. Paul and St. George, along with tiny, uninhabited Otter and Walrus Islands, make up the Pribilof Island group.

Of all Alaska Native groups, the Aleuts have had the longest history of mingling cultures with non-Natives, ever since the mid-1700s. Rediscovering their Aleut identity has become a passion for many islanders, including Katiana.

With help from parents and grandparents, Katiana, her brothers, and her friends are learning Aleut history, language, and arts in summertime culture camps and in school as an elective. Katiana's mother, Aquilina, is one of the leaders.

The Pribilofs lie 150 miles north of the ancestral home of all Aleuts, the Aleutian Islands, a thousand-mile arc of 200 islands. People migrated there centuries ago from mainland Alaska. Their route likely began in Asia and crossed the Bering Land Bridge, which once connected North America with Asia. The oldest Aleut settlement is 8,400 years old.

◄ *The tundra comes alive with wildflowers each spring.* ▲ *Just outside town is a beach where northern fur seals spend their summers. Katiana and her friends must watch from a distance because the seals are protected by federal law.*

Katiana and her friend Samantha Zacharof share a laugh at the community center, where a skin-sewing class is under way.

People have lived in the Pribilofs, however, for just over 200 years, when the ancestors of today's residents were taken there. Russian fur traders, the *promyshlenniki,* needed laborers to harvest seals for the pelts, so they enslaved Aleut men.

There are no trees on the Aleutians or the Pribilofs, just wild grass that grows plentifully and wind that blows at a constant ten to twenty miles per hour. It's often rainy, foggy, and mild. The average winter day is about thirty degrees, with summers in the upper forties.

A herd of imported reindeer roams St. Paul Island, and its cliffs are the nesting grounds for more than two million seabirds, including horned puffins and red-legged kittiwakes. Blue foxes sneak around, trying to steal eggs. Seals spend summers on the beach. The harbor is full of commercial fishing boats. And everywhere, it seems, there are sand dunes for kids to play on.

"I love jumping off sand dunes," Katiana says, "and especially rolling down them." Growing up in a place where she knows everyone, Katiana says she feels safe and free to wander. She also likes writing letters, staying up late and telling scary stories, and playing card games.

Nearly everyone on St. Paul is Aleut, and, like Katiana, nearly everyone has a Russian name and attends the Russian Orthodox church, a whitewashed building adorned with three Russian crosses. Today, to be Aleut is to be Russian Orthodox. Parts of the two cultures have become inseparably entwined.

Before the Russians came to the Aleutians, as many as 15,000 Aleuts were part of a well-defined culture oriented to the sea. The ocean provided food and clothing. Women used dried grasses to weave intricate baskets. The *kamleika,* the Aleut raincoat, was made from naturally waterproof seal gut. With the Russians came Western-style clothing, above-ground frame houses, and Christian beliefs. Also war and disease. Aleut numbers plummeted from 10,000 in the late 1700s to about 4,000 a century later. Now there are about 2,000 Aleuts.

Katiana, who hopes to be a teacher someday, is an avid student of Aleut history.

"I want to learn the stories of the Aleuts so I can pass them on to my children and grandchildren," says Katiana, who lives with her mother and two teenage brothers.

"I mostly learn from my mom, my Aleut teacher, and my grandparents," she says. "In school, I wish I could learn just four subjects: social studies, science, Aleut, and Russian."

Few textbooks include what happened to Katiana's village during World War II. In June 1942, before Alaska was a state, Japanese planes bombed the Aleutians, and the U.S. government decided to move all remaining Aleuts to safety. Everyone in St. Paul was relocated to an abandoned cannery in Southeast Alaska, where many fell ill and died from poor sanitation and disease. At war's end, survivors returned to find their homes had been occupied by the military. Katiana's home was one of them. Some had been vandalized.

Not until the mid-1980s were the Aleuts finally repaid for their wartime losses. Some felt that no amount of money could make up for what had happened.

One overcast afternoon, Katiana leads the way to a beach, where a seal blind has been erected near the road. Visitors can view the seals through slots in the wooden screen without disturbing them. Although the federal government oversaw a seal harvest operation for decades, today the seals are protected by the U.S. Fish and Wildlife Service, and the Aleuts are allowed enough to feed themselves.

"All I can say is seal meat is delicious," says Katiana. Her favorite part: "Eating the liver and roasting the heart. You put it on a stick or a hanger and just cook it over the fire. I like it good and crispy."

Katiana and her mom, Aquilina, are especially close. Aquilina and other St. Paul parents are helping their children learn more about Aleut culture.

The napping seals are nearly indistinguishable from the dark boulders beneath and around them, until one of them wriggles, its flesh rippling, to find a more comfortable spot. Behind the blind, a carpet of vegetation rises from the road uphill to a higher lookout point, and Katiana scrambles up, searching for *pushki*, or wild celery.

"It's nice and juicy," she says. "It makes me feel the Native inside. I think about the early Aleuts."

Elsewhere on the island, Katiana points out a deep, grassy indentation in the ground. It marks the caved-in remains of a *barabara*, a semi-underground home for ten to forty Aleut families. Nearby, on a point from which you can see both sides of the island at once, a Russian Orthodox cross has been erected.

Like this place, Katiana pays homage to both branches of her family tree—Russian and Aleut— but inside, she says, she'll always be one of the *Unangan*, the word Aleuts use to describe themselves: The People.

4

The
Ocean
Feeds
Our
Family

Selina Tolson HAIDA

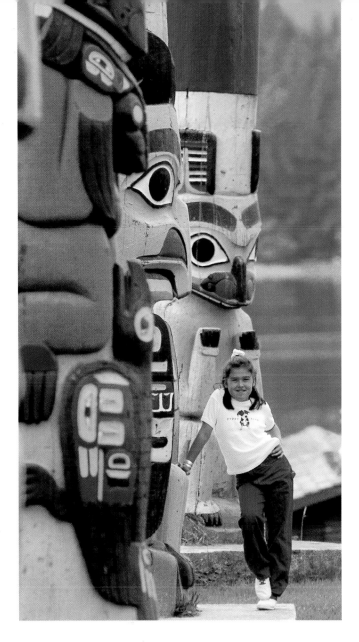

Belly down on the Hydaburg dock, Selina Tolson, nine, and her cousin Jamie peer into the shadowy water beneath them. The girls identify seaweed, jellyfish, and salmon while they wait for Selina's teenage brother Charles to come with his skiff. Selina's family left earlier on the *Haida Girl*, her grandfather's fifty-six-foot commercial seiner, and the girls are anxious to join them at a picnic across the water.

"Look at those fish!" says Selina. "I wish I had my brother's rod." She loves to fish for salmon, although she admits that a brother helps reel them in. Selina has three brothers and two sisters, a cat named Fatso, a pen pal, a treehouse, and a *chanáa*, or grandfather, who tells her wonderful stories.

This late August day is sunny and dry, a rare occasion. Hydaburg, a village of about 400 Haida Indian people, lies in rain forest country on Prince of Wales Island in Southeast Alaska. Each year, the area normally gets about 150 inches of rain and a little snow.

Minutes pass slowly. The girls roll onto their backs to stare at the clouds. On Selina's wrist are two broad, engraved silver bracelets that tinkle whenever they touch. The Eagle clan symbol adorns one. Selina wears a silver ring too.

"My uncle gave me this ring," Selina says. "This bracelet was my dad's mother's, and when she died, he gave it to me. I don't take them off, ever."

Artistically, the Haidas have much in common with their neighbors, the Tlingits and Tsimshians. Their styles vary so slightly that only a clan member or a fellow artist might notice the differences. All three groups carve totem poles and follow similar customs in clan organization. But each group retains its own identity and tribal lore, and each is known for its artistic specialty. Historically, for the Haidas, it was dugout canoes, made from the biggest cedar trees in the region—found about forty miles south on Canada's Queen Charlotte Islands.

◄ *A member of the Eagle clan, Selina models her ceremonial regalia.* ▲ *Rows of totem poles stand next to Selina's school. Some are new poles; others are very old, collected from other places on the island.*

Selina loves to fish. Although she'd rather have a coho salmon on the end of her line, she'll settle for this rockfish.

In Selina's village there is an abundance of artists. Rosa Alby makes beautiful button blankets. Her brother, Warren, carves Haida-style boats and totems. Viola Burgess teaches Haida art to the children. Selina's mom, Christine, is among those who teach Haida dance.

"Our dance costume is a special blanket with our clan on it," says Selina. "Jamie and I are Eagle. There's Eagle, Frog, Bullhead, and Beaver.

"We don't use the same dance steps for every song," she explains. "We practice what we're going to do. And our teachers teach us Haida words, like *kwáadaa*. That means 'quarter,' and *dáalaa* means 'money,' and *dúus* means 'cat.' *Háw'aa* means 'thank you.'"

Next to Selina's school is a grassy lot lined with totem poles. Life in a rain forest means there are always plenty of large trees for carving. The frequent rain and constant dampness speed the natural decay of these valuable pieces of history and art. Some were moved from other places on Prince of Wales; others were carved here. Historically, the totems served as storytellers, memorials, or signs of clan ownership.

Finally, Selina spots Charles on the horizon and jumps to her feet. Within minutes, he motors in and helps his passengers aboard for a twenty-minute ride.

At the picnic, three generations of adults— Selina's aunts, uncles, grandparents, older cousins, and family friends—sit on driftwood logs, talking, laughing, and feeding a bonfire. Over the flames, they roast hot dogs and marshmallows. Tupperware containers of salads, smoked *chíin*, or salmon, and desserts are opened. A few grown-ups keep their eyes on the young ones romping in the chilly ocean. Selina can't be tempted to jump in, but wades instead, squealing when the cold water laps against her ankles.

Occasionally, a shivering child runs up to a parent for a rubdown with a towel. A few head into the woods to look for berries. Seated in nearby lawn chairs are Selina's grandparents, Sylvester and Frieda Peele, respected tribal elders who are passing on stories, language, and dance, teaching the Haida ways in daily life and in cultural heritage classes for children.

Sylvester was born in Hydaburg, but his parents were not. His mother came from British Columbia, and his father was from Klinkwan, a village about ten or twelve miles away from Hydaburg. Klinkwan and another village were abandoned in 1911 when the government forced the residents to move to Hydaburg.

"It was mostly for school purposes," Sylvester says gently. "But this was a better place to live, with a river and lots of salmon." At one time his ancestors

Selina poses with her mother, Christine, and grandparents Sylvester and Frieda Peele. Because clan membership is passed from mother to child, Frieda, Christine, and Selina are all Eagles.

all lived in Canada. Some tribal stories say that about 400 years ago there was a food shortage, and one group came north to Prince of Wales Island.

The Alaska Haidas settled in villages that had been abandoned by Tlingits. However, other storytellers say the new arrivals warred with the Tlingits, driving them to the northern part of the island. Today, an invisible boundary splits the island, with Tlingit country in the north and the Haidas in the south. But wars? None lately.

The Haidas found plentiful food when they arrived: deer, berries, fish eggs, crab, salmon, halibut, and seaweed. And even though Hydaburg's children can walk to the little Do Drop grocery store for candy, pop, crackers, or other snacks, their families still mostly rely on the ocean to feed them.

"I like coho eggs and dog salmon eggs," says Selina. "We dry them and save them for the winter. I help pick the berries, and I help with drying seaweed, too.

"My brothers usually go out on the boat and get seaweed on the beach somewhere. At home, they grind it up in the grinder and lay it out on the roof of the house to dry. Then we seal it in plastic bags."

The picnic is wrapping up, and as mothers and aunties are replacing lids and gathering children, the men fold up chairs and carry supplies to the water's edge.

In the middle of the cove, the beautiful *Haida Girl* waits, anchored in the still, gray water. Charles shuttles the party from the beach to the seiner, a handful at a time. Voyaging home to Hydaburg, Selina turns her face toward the bow of the *Haida Girl*. Her long, black hair flutters in the wind like a flag.

5
Russian
Christmas
on the
Kuskokwim
River

Andrea Hoelscher

YUP'IK

It's two o'clock in the morning and twelve-year-old Andrea Hoelscher is bleary-eyed, but she's still on her feet in the custom of her church, with men on the right and women on the left. Today is January 7—Russian Christmas in Lower Kalskag, a Yup'ik Eskimo village on the Kuskokwim River in Southwest Alaska.

Services are sung or chanted by the priest and a small choir, led by Andrea's Grandma Ida, in a mix of English, Yup'ik, and Slavonic, a form of Old Russian. Andrea's mother, Molly, is a singer; her stepdad, Mickey Nicolai, is standing among the men.

Nearly everyone in this village of 300 people is a member of the Russian Orthodox Church, which observes its holy days by an ancient calendar. Christmas here is called *Selavi*, and is celebrated

with all-night church, fireworks, and seven nights of "starring" until January 14, Russian New Year's. Each night, the villagers form a house-to-house parade behind two decorated, glittering stars—one for children and one for adults.

"Mary and Joseph went to Bethlehem, where Jesus was born, and the wise men followed the star," Andrea says. "So we walk from house to house and go in for awhile. The person holding the star twirls it, and we sing. In some houses, we eat. People give presents."

The holiday has been observed in parts of Alaska since the early Russians arrived in the mid-1700s. In time, Russian Orthodox missionaries brought their faith to the Native population—primarily the Aleuts,

◄ *Wearing a fur hat against below-zero temperatures, Andrea stops to pet a loose puppy.* ▲ *In Andrea's church, Christmas is celebrated on January 7; New Year's is January 14.*

Andrea bends to kiss a holy icon during the Christmas service. While the outside of Andrea's church may be plain, the inside is full of beautiful old religious paintings, lights, linens, and silver.

Tlingits, and coastal Yup'iks. Some inland river communities eventually were converted, among them Lower Kalskag.

Another Kalskag—Upper Kalskag—lies upriver about three miles. Local people shorten the village names to Upper and Lower. They share a grade school in Upper and a high school in Lower. For groceries and sundries, a variety of home-based mom-and-pop stores round out the local diet of fish and game.

Andrea's people, the Yup'iks, are the major group of the Yuut, or southern Eskimos, which include smaller groups such as the Koniags, Alutiiqs, and Chugach. Customs vary with the environment. Sea mammals are important to islanders and those on the Bering Sea Coast. Inland villages on the big rivers of Southwestern Alaska—including Lower Kalskag—rely on salmon, whitefish, moose, and caribou.

Today, about sixty Yup'ik villages of 100 to 500 people populate the Yukon-Kuskokwim Delta. About 80 percent speak Yup'ik as a first language. Villagers on the rivers get around by snowmachine

or four-wheeler in winter, when the Kuskokwim River is a frozen highway. Even cars and trucks drive the river. Summer river traffic is equally busy, with skiffs buzzing around at all hours under the Midnight Sun.

Each summer, Andrea and her family move away from their log cabin home and board their twenty-foot boat for a three-mile ride downriver to their fish camp. There they spend the season stocking up on fish to last the winter.

"We stay as long as we can—a week and a half or so. When we run out of supplies, we come home, get more, and go back," says Andrea's stepdad, Mickey, who carves ivory, moose horn, bone, and baleen to supplement his income.

The family's fifty-foot set net hangs in the water like a curtain attached to floats, and the men and boys pull it up and "pick fish." The Yup'ik women and girls spend long hours with their *ulus* on tables near the river, cleaning and cutting fish into strips to dry, smoke, or can.

"Fish camp is like camping, but you have to work—cut fish, rake, clean up," Andrea says. "I cut dog salmon, whitefish, Dolly Varden, king salmon, silver salmon. For my grandma most of the time. She puts up lots of fish. My *apa* [grandfather] always catches lots."

Artistically, the Yup'iks are perhaps best known for their distinctive mask making and dancing. As the drummers beat and chant, women in shirt-dresses, called *qaspeqs*, and beaded headgear keep their feet planted and rhythmically gesture with dance fans made of woven grass, fur, and beads.

The men are vigorous dancers, crouching, standing on one foot, and stomping the other with the beat as their arms play out the drama of a story. Their dance gloves are beaded and fur-lined. Sometimes the dancers wear stylized masks of bone or wood, trimmed with feathers, to tell their dance stories.

Andrea is learning about her ancestors' customs in cultural heritage class, a school elective, and her Grandma Ida is among those teaching her how to speak Yup'ik.

"Our teachers and the elders tell us stories about a long time ago, and that's pretty interesting," Andrea says. "We learn how to bead and how to skin rabbits and sew skins."

In Lower, the Russian Orthodox Church has replaced the spiritual practices of Andrea's ancestors, who believed in reincarnation and that humans and animals all had souls. And, as happened elsewhere in Alaska, this influence of missionaries as well as Western teachers discouraged traditional spiritual expression, especially dancing, and the public practice was absent in Kalskag for two generations.

"We almost lost it," says Andrea's mother, "but the two villages are getting together and helping each other out. There's only one elder I know who's teaching the children the words of the songs and

At the edge of the Kuskokwim River, the basketball court is plowed and ready for players, even in winter. Andrea tries some snowball basketball.

the drumming." Other Yup'ik villages are seeing strong revivals in dancing and traditional spiritual teaching; however, in Lower, in keeping with the Russian Orthodox teachings, the dances aren't reflecting the old, non-Christian beliefs, Molly says. Not unless the dancer is at home, dancing privately.

It's five in the morning, and the Christmas service is ending. Slow-moving worshippers hug and wish each other "Merry Christmas" as they zip their parkas and slip on beaver hats. The fire will go out in the church's wood stove, and the villagers will go home to catch a few hours of sleep before the night's festivities. And for once, Andrea can't wait to go to bed.

6

I'm Happy
To Be an
Island Boy

Danny Hewson
TSIMSHIAN

Just outside Danny Hewson's door in Metlakatla, on Annette Island, the chill of a late-summer morning is scented with cedar. Pale yellow shavings spill out of his dad's art studio. Throughout Southeast Alaska, Wayne Hewson is rapidly gaining respect for his totem poles, masks, paintings, prints, and dance regalia.

Danny, eleven, once carved a ladle, and while he's proud of his father, he doesn't feel drawn to the life of a master carver himself. Instead, he wants to find a job, maybe at the market where his mother, Toni, and sixteen-year-old brother, David, work. Mainly, he wants to marry and stay on this remote island seventeen miles southeast of Ketchikan.

Wayne has something different in mind. "I'm going to try to encourage my sons to leave," he says. "Although they could have a life here, it's a whole different world out there—even just in Ketchikan. Right here, it's just us."

Annette Island is the only Tsimshian land in Alaska. Almost all of its 2,000 residents are descended from Indians who migrated north from Canada in 1887 with Father William Duncan, a missionary for the Episcopal Church of England. The Tsimshians were divided. About 800 joined him; even more stayed behind in Canada. The churchman discouraged the Natives from practicing their traditional art and customs.

"Father Duncan wasn't a bad man," says Wayne. "He did a lot of wonderful things for our people. But he made the people stop their practices because he thought they were evil. He thought we were worshipping the totem poles, but they were story poles—we didn't have a written language."

The place where Father Duncan settled is beautiful. So far south, Metlakatla enjoys a mild climate, even in winter. The village is dwarfed by mountains and bordered by stands of giant spruce, cedar, and hemlock trees. To the west are the steely blue waters of the Inside Passage.

In most rural Alaskan villages, dirt or gravel

◀ *The carvings of Wayne Hewson, Danny's dad, are found all over Metlakatla.* ▲ *In the studio, Danny helps chisel out big sections of wood before his dad carves in the details.*

Commercial fishing boats fill Metlakatla's small boat harbor.

roads and natural yards are the norm. Here, kids ride bikes and roller-blade on paved streets. There are curbs and sidewalks, and neat lawns are bordered with fences. Basketball hoops face the street.

Alaska Marine Highway System ferries call here every Thursday and Saturday. Soon cruise ships will be stopping, and the Metlakatlans hope that tourism dollars will boost their economy. A sawmill and a cannery employ many people, and there is a handful of small businesses and restaurants. Most residents shop for school or Christmas through the J. C. Penney catalog. There are no street signs, and no strangers who can't be accounted for.

Near the entrance to the senior center is a totem pole that Wayne carved. It tells a story that Danny can't remember.

"The bottom figure is Bear," says Danny, "and the top figure is Killer Whale. There's a face on each side. One side has a woman, and one side has a man. You can tell it's a woman because a long time ago, women used to put things in their lips—a *labret* that pierced their lower lip—and it used to sag down

like that. And the bottom figure is the Bear."

Danny explains that while most totems are story poles, his people also used to carve mortuary poles. "They used to put this little hole at the back of the totem pole. And when someone died, they'd make a bentwood box, break the bones and fold them inside of it, and then burn the box and put it all inside the totem pole. Outsiders thought they were worshipping the totem pole, but they were honoring the person who was inside there."

Danny likes to ride his bike down to the boat harbor and scramble over the large boulders of the breakwater. Some days, he snacks on salmonberries and huckleberries as he hikes out to Pioneer Park, where he likes to swing on a rope over the incoming tide. He built a fort in his backyard, and he's thinking about an overnight. It's as if the island is his playground.

In Danny's pocket is a new mail-order Swiss Army knife that just arrived. He takes it out every so often to examine it.

"You could survive in the woods with this,"

A piece of driftwood, a long rope, and a tall spruce tree are a formula for fun as Danny swings out over the water.

Danny says as he fiddles with the knife's seventeen functions—including blades, scissors, toothpick, and a miniature saw. "You could make a shelter!"

Danny's island has been a reservation since the U.S. Congress created it in 1891. When Native land rights were decided in the Alaska Native Claims Settlement Act of 1971, Annette Island was not included. It remained a reservation.

"Any Alaska Native who's not part of Land Claims is welcome here," says Wayne. "It belongs to free Native people."

Tsimshian regulations dictate that even a free Native person must reside one year to become a "member" of the reservation. Because Danny's mother is non-Native, she must reapply every year for permission to live on the island. She can't own land, and she can't buy a house.

And, like the Tlingits, Tsimshian society follows a matriarchal clan line, so Danny and his brother were born without a clan symbol.

"My sons don't have an Alaska crest because their mother is non-Native," Wayne says. "We are what our mothers are. My mom was Killer Whale, so I'm Killer Whale."

However, David Boxley, a close friend and Wayne's carving mentor, adopted the Hewson boys into his Eagle clan at a potlatch a few years ago. Like other Alaska Natives, the Tsimshians are experiencing a reawakening of their traditional culture, including the revival of potlatches and the Tsimshian language, the making of dance regalia, and the carving of new masks and totems.

The revival began in Metlakatla in the 1980s as young people, curious about the old ways, began asking questions of village elders and Tsimshian relatives in Canada. Today, the Alaska Tsimshians gather often for potlatches with feasting, naming ceremonies, clan adoptions, dancing, storytelling, and totem raisings. The whole village seems to be learning together, several generations at once. And Danny, for one, is an eager student, especially of drumming.

"The Tsimshian tribe is coming alive," he says, "and I want to be part of it."

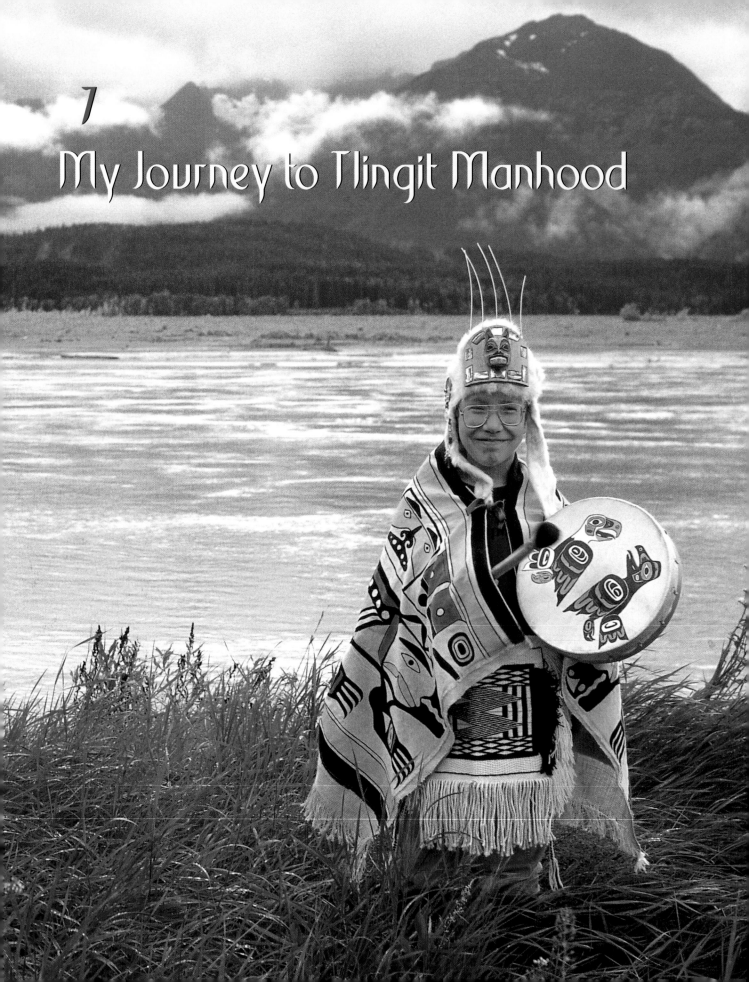

7

My Journey to Tlingit Manhood

Josh Hotch

Josh Hotch doesn't know whom he'll marry when he grows up, but he knows she'll be a Raven, so his children will be Ravens. That's because Josh is a member of the other Tlingit clan—the Eagle clan—just like his mother.

"You are what your mother is," he explains. "An Eagle can't marry an Eagle, and a Raven can't marry a Raven." Marrying within your clan would be like marrying a member of your family.

At ten, Josh may not know the word *moiety*, but he understands the concept. Throughout Tlingit territory—nearly all of Alaska's Southeast Panhandle—the Natives historically were born into two moieties, or membership groups, called Eagle and Raven, and further divided into subclans with animal symbols such as Killer Whale, Wolf, or Frog.

The clans shared responsibilities. If one clan organized to build a house, the other clan finished the work. Then the first hosted a potlatch, a ceremonial feast that focused on gift-giving, memorials, and displays of wealth. If a clan member died, the other clan prepared the dead for cremation or burial. Later, the deceased's clan would show their thanks by hosting a potlatch. And so it went, back and forth, sharing labor and gifts, with each clan helping and honoring the other.

These customs are among the ancient Tlingit traditions woven into daily life in Klukwan, Josh's home village of 140 people in the northern part of the state's Panhandle. So, too, are practices such as smoking and drying fish, carving totem poles and masks, weaving Raven's Tail robes and Chilkat

◄ *Josh is robed in a Chilkat blanket, part of his dance regalia.* ▲ *Josh and his uncle, Albert Paddy, leave the village for a fish site on the Chilkat River.*

37

Klukwan is so small that there are ten children in Josh's class of second- through fourth-graders.

blankets, dancing and singing, storytelling, and celebrating in potlatches. Nothing is done for the sake of tourists—it's just everyday living. The residents also drive cars and own fax machines in a village that mixes past and present in a postcard setting.

"Klukwan is a nice place," says Josh. "We have the biggest mountains in the U.S.A. We have evergreen and cottonwood trees and glaciers. Salmon, fish, and deer, too. In the spring, the hooligan are here—they're the teeny fish that you can't catch in salmon fishing nets. We make hooligan oil out of them. We dip dried fish or dried hooligan in it—it's a snack!"

Klukwan is indeed a beautiful, bountiful place to live. That's probably why Chilkat Tlingits have lived in this valley for thousands of years. They were sophisticated artisans who often traded with their Athabascan neighbors. They also held the rights to the trails later used by Gold Rush prospectors headed for the Klondike.

At the edge of Josh's backyard, beyond the swing set and the fringe of cottonwoods, beyond the smokehouse and the skiff, the Chilkat River rolls by in a broad, braided pattern. In the distance, snow-capped mountains tower above a lush, green valley teeming with fish and wildlife.

The people of Klukwan depend on fish and game as their food staples, and drive twenty-one miles to Haines for any other groceries, to pick up mail, see a movie, or board the ferry on the Inside Passage.

The villagers share this valley with the largest gathering of bald eagles in North America. Each October and November, up to 4,000 eagles congregate to glut themselves on late-run salmon in the Chilkat River.

"Eagles fight with eagles for the fish," Josh says.

Josh's village is long and narrow, laid out parallel to the river along one unpaved street with weathered cabins and newer frame homes sprinkled on each side. Near the middle is the community center, used for potlatches and other special events. Josh and his cousins like to explore, run, play hide-and-seek, and go bike riding around town. There's plenty of room and little traffic. And everybody knows everybody else.

Even though Josh is still young, he has learned the rules of his society, not from books, but from the Ravens and Eagles around him. And if he'd been born a century ago, he would have practiced another Tlingit tradition, the "avunculate." At about age six, Tlingit boys used to go live with their mother's brother, who taught them as they grew to manhood. It was believed that fathers would be too easy on their sons, but that an uncle was the right combination of softness and strictness.

Josh's dad, Jones, is a tribal government leader who's teaching his son with assistance from a special uncle. Today, Tlingit children don't leave home for the avunculate, but uncles still help to instruct them, and not just the boys in the family. When Josh's mom, Lani, was growing up, she and her brothers learned from their mother's brother, Albert Paddy. And when Josh was born, Lani gave him Uncle Albert's Tlingit name: *Kaan-kai-da.*

"He still watches out for us now, even though we're grown," Lani says. "And he's been training Josh on the fishing boat on the river. He also had an important role in showing me how to make dried fish, along with my grandmother, my mom, and my dad."

Contact with non-Native settlers, gold miners, missionaries, and educators in the last two centuries has altered the ancient ways of the Tlingit people. Especially in the 1900s, the loss of traditional dancing, singing, and weaving was sorely felt.

"Josh's grandparents weren't taught to dance and sing," Lani says. "If they used their language, they were punished." And as old weavers died, few young people were trained to follow. Only in the last decade has Lani's generation learned the songs and dances of their ancestors by listening to old recordings and experimenting with movements. "We had a lot of encouragement from the elders," she says.

From the adults around him, Josh has learned the meaning of the symbols on totem poles and on his special dance clothing. He's learned how to bead, dance, sing, and prepare salmon for smoking.

"You cut off the head, tail, and fins," Josh says. "You use cottonwood to burn in the smokehouse. There's a screen so that no bugs can get in. It's just like how it sounds: dried fish would be dry; smoked fish would taste like smoke. What I like are herring eggs. They're crunchy. They're better than potato chips!"

On his way to becoming a man, Josh is surrounded by a village full of Eagles and Ravens who will make sure he knows who is he: *Kaan-kai-da,* a Tlingit, a son of Klukwan.

▲ ▲ *Josh uses a spotting scope to watch for eagles in trees along the river.* ▲ *Cocoa, Josh's Labrador retriever, begs for some highbush cranberries.*

8

Bright
Lights and
My Big
Village

Tauni Thompson
ALEUT–CAUCASIAN

Like most young girls in Anchorage, eleven-year-old Tauni Thompson likes to ride her bike or go sledding, eat at McDonald's, and shop at the Fifth Avenue Mall. Tauni considers herself a city girl. And yet, even though her family lives in a community of a quarter-million people, the Alaska wilderness remains a powerful influence, and it's just minutes away.

Living in a modern neighborhood hasn't made the Thompson family too citified. Like hundreds of families in Anchorage, they live a subsistence lifestyle, meaning they still depend on hunting and fishing to fill their freezer. The grocery store supplies the rest of their needs.

In summers, the Thompsons—parents Carl and Andrea, and children Beverly, Tauni, Allen, and John—may drive hundreds of miles to dip-net for salmon. Every fall, Tauni's family takes a skiff across Cook Inlet to a little cabin they own in the wilderness. There they spend weekends, or sometimes longer, without running water or electricity as they hunt for ducks and big game.

"My dad goes moose hunting in the fall," Tauni says, "so we eat moose meat a lot. I went duck hunting a couple years, but never got anything. Dad says when I was about five, he'd take me hunting and I'd fall asleep. When I heard shooting, I'd wake up, go get the duck, and come back and go to sleep again."

Tauni's town, Anchorage, was founded in 1915 as a tent city for workers building the Alaska Railroad. Early Alaskans who lived in this region were Tanaina Athabascans, who considered the Anchorage area too marshy for any permanent settlement. Railroad builders made camp anyway. Today Anchorage is Alaska's biggest city—about half the state's population lives there.

Anchorage also is home to the largest concentration of Alaska Natives anywhere—about 20,000. Some new arrivals from rural Alaska, called "the Bush," are overwhelmed by the tall buildings, four-lane traffic, and urban sprawl. Each fall, villagers and urban Natives alike gather in Anchorage for the annual meeting of the Alaska Federation of Natives, a political and cultural conference. In February, it's

◄ *Tauni loves playing in the snow but finds fun in every season.* ▲ *Tauni explores the gardens of Anchorage's Town Square, next to the Alaska Center for the Performing Arts.*

41

Tauni enjoys duck hunting with her dad, and she's learning how to safely handle his 12-gauge shotgun.

Fur Rendezvous, a week-long winter carnival with a parade, fur auction, craft fair, and other events that attract hundreds of visitors from the Bush.

Tauni is part Aleut, the Alaska Native group that suffered the greatest cultural loss when non-Natives began arriving in the mid-1700s. Her Aleut grandparents and their eight children grew up on the Alaska Peninsula among Yup'ik Eskimos, further mingling cultures.

"I didn't grow up in what people view as the traditional Native way," says Tauni's mother. "It's just the way my parents raised us. They didn't eat much beaver, whale, seal, or Native food. Mostly just big game—caribou, moose—or ducks and geese."

Tauni remembers the summer camp she attended a few years ago where Native kids were taught about Alaska's various cultures. "We learned Eskimo dances, like the seal hunt and an igloo dance. Some kids made a dancing stick; some did soapstone carving. I like to draw. I've been drawing since I was about three—mostly things from nature, like animals, trees, and mountains."

While Tauni respects her roots, ancient Aleut traditions are not as important to her as just being Alaskan and learning subsistence ways and outdoor skills from her parents. For a city girl, she's well trained in survival.

"If I got lost in the woods, I'd probably stay in one place until someone came for me," Tauni says. "I'd probably make a little shelter, so no animals could hurt me, and start a fire."

Tauni's dad is a Caucasian man whose parents came from Idaho to homestead in Alaska. They settled on ten acres near Cook Inlet in 1952 and showed their children how to live off the land. There were no roads to the Thompson place back then, but Anchorage kept growing and eventually surrounded the land of the homestead. Medical expenses forced Tauni's grandparents to sell much of their property until just their home and three-quarters of an acre were left.

Today, Tauni and her family live in the old house on land that's still as wild as it was forty years ago. But beyond their property, a modern subdivision

A whale mural by Hawaiian artist Wyland decorates the side of a department store in downtown Anchorage.

has sprouted, with single-family homes in rows of groomed lots.

Tauni's second home is Egegik, a commercial fishing village on the Bristol Bay side of the Alaska Peninsula. There are no roads to Egegik. Most seasonal residents fly in or arrive by boat. The waters of Bristol Bay are the richest salmon fishing grounds in the state, and every summer Egegik explodes from a sleepy village of about 70 people into a bustling fishing town of about 1,500.

Before her Aleut grandparents retired from commercial fishing, Tauni used to visit Egegik during fishing season with hopes that her Grandma Nida would make Eskimo ice cream.

"My grandma makes good *akutaq*," Tauni says. "It's made of berries, Crisco, and sugar. Sometimes people put seal oil in it."

Since the heavy-duty fishing work was left for adults and teenagers, Tauni's Egegik days were filled with creative playtime.

"We'd mostly ride four-wheelers around or walk," Tauni says. "We'd go to the docks and look at the boats. They pull the salmon onto the boat, and then they throw back the ones that are too small, and the crabs and flounders and stuff they're not supposed to catch during salmon season."

As pleasant as Egegik is, Tauni prefers Anchorage because "there's more lights and stuff." After school, she can walk to Jewel Lake for ice skating and ice fishing. Beyond her house is a trail down the bluff to the flats of Cook Inlet. Traveling south out of Anchorage, she can see Dall sheep, eagles, moose, or beluga whales right from her car window.

And just a few miles away are popular hiking trails. A sawed-off mountain named Flattop is a destination for many Anchorage families, like Tauni's, who love the outdoors.

"Going up Flattop," Tauni says, "it's mostly trails, and then there's about a hundred feet of rock. From the top you can see the buildings of Anchorage. I like to go when the sun is just setting because it's a blue-peachy color. It's so pretty. I wouldn't want to live in any other state besides Alaska."

Glossary

Children in the Pribilof Island dance group.

An ulu *and* maktaq.

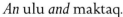

aġvig (Iñupiaq): Bowhead whale.

atigi (Iñupiaq): Parka.

baleen: The hairy plates (black, horn-like) hanging from the bowhead's upper jaw that filter sea organisms from the water, feeding the whale. Today, Iñupiat artists use baleen mostly for weaving or carving.

ignig (Iñupiaq): fire.

iglu (Iñupiaq): Any house or dwelling—not just an ice house. Dome-shaped houses made of ice bricks used only as emergency shelters. English spelling is *igloo*.

Iñupiaq: Singular of Iñupiat, but often used in English for the name of the language.

Iñupiat: Plural word for the Eskimo Native group that has inhabited Alaska's northernmost region for many thousands of years.

maktaq (Iñupiaq): The two-inch layer of whale skin and twelve inches of blubber beneath it. English spelling is *muktuk*.

nanuq (Iñupiaq): Polar bear. English spelling is *nanook*.

ugruk (Iñupiaq): Bearded seal.

ulu (Iñupiaq): Women's knife used for skinning, cooking, and sewing.

Athabascan: Indian group that occupies the Interior and some parts of Southcentral Alaska.

ch'etth'ena' (Lower Tanana Athabascan): Dentalium, the decorative white shells that are sewn onto tunics and fashioned into necklaces, bracelets, and headbands.

denèegee (Lower Tanana Athabascan): Moose.

deyenenh (Lower Tanana Athabascan): A medicine man (shaman), the intercessor between the physical and spiritual worlds.

dzen (Lower Tanana Athabascan): Muskrat.

44

ganhok (Lower Tanana Athabascan): The carved wooden dance stick—decorated with large beads and yarn tassels—that is raised and lowered at potlatch dances to control the sound level.

snow-go: The term used by many Bush residents for a snowmachine or snowmobile.

3

Aleut: Native group that lives in the Pribilof Islands and along the 1,000-mile arc of islands known as the Aleutian Chain.

barabara (English spelling of Russian word): A traditional Aleut semi-subterranean home, built to hold ten to forty families.

kamleika (English spelling of Russian word): Marine-mammal gut parka used as a waterproof garment.

promyshlenniki (Russian): Fur hunters and traders (literally means "enterprisers").

pushki (Russian): Wild celery.

Unangan (Aleut): The term Aleuts use to refer to themselves as a people.

4

chanáa (Haida): Grandfather.

chíin (Haida): Salmon.

dáalaa (Chinook slang): Money.

dúus (May be from Chinook slang pus-pus for "puss"): Cat.

Haida: Indian group that lives on the southern half of Prince of Wales Island in Southeast Alaska.

háw'aa (Haida): Thank you.

kwáadaa (Chinook slang): Quarter.

5

apa (Yup'ik): Grandfather.

qaspeq (Yup'ik): Casual, colorful shirtdress with a hood and flounce. English spelling is *kuspuk*.

Selavi (Yup'ik): Russian Christmas. English spelling is *Slaviq*.

Slavonic: A form of Old Russian used in Russian Orthodox Church services.

starring: The Russian Orthodox tradition in which a party of carolers follows twirling stars through the streets, stopping to sing and share food or small gifts at houses along the way.

Yup'ik: Literally, the "real people." English spelling is *Yupik*. Eskimo group that lives in Alaska's southwestern region, including coastal areas, islands, and along the Yukon and Kuskokwim Rivers.

6

bentwood box: A box with all four sides made from one piece of wood that has been notched, steamed, bent, and bound together.

labret: A decorative, button-like piece of metal or wood worn in a pierced lip or cheek.

mortuary poles: Totem poles that contained cremated remains.

regalia: Clothing, slippers, gloves, and headgear worn on special occasions or for dancing.

Tsimshian: Indian group that lives on Annette Island in Southeast Alaska.

Athabascan beaded moccasins are made from moosehide.

Chilkat blankets feature Tlingit clan symbols.

7

avunculate: The Tlingit practice in which a boy was trained by his mother's brother; boys usually left home at about age six to live with their uncles.

Chilkat blanket: A patterned blanket woven from strips of bark and mountain goat hair and worn over the shoulders. Traditionally, Tlingit men created the designs on pattern boards, which women used as guides for their weaving.

hooligan: Small, greasy fish also known as eulachon or candlefish. Hooligan are dried and eaten, or rendered for oil that is used for dipping or burned for light.

moiety: The division of a society into two tribal subdivisions. The two groups in Tlingit society are Raven and Eagle/Wolf. For Tlingits, membership is passed from mother to child.

potlatch: A ceremonial feast focused on gift-giving, memorials, and displays of wealth.

Raven's Tail robe: A prized, hand-woven covering in a distinctive black-and-white pattern that looks something like the overlapping feathers of a bird's tail.

Tlingit: The largest of the three Southeast Indian groups, the Tlingits claim nearly all of Alaska's Panhandle.

8

akutaq (Yup'ik): Eskimo ice cream, made with berries, sugar, and Crisco (or seal oil). English spelling is *agutuk*.

Bush: Any remote region of Alaska that is not connected to the road system.

dip-net: To fish with a long-handled net while standing in the river.

Yup'ik families dry fish to eat later.

Recommended Reading

Josh Hotch attends the Klukwan School.

Brown, Emily Ivanoff. 1981. *Roots of Ticasuk: An Eskimo Woman's Family Story*. Seattle: Alaska Northwest Books.

Chandonnet, Ann. 1989. *Chief Stephen's Parky: One Year in the Life of an Athapascan Girl*. Billings, Mont.: Council for Indian Education.

Green, Paul, and Abbe Abbott. 1959. *I Am Eskimo: Aknik My Name*. Seattle: Alaska Northwest Books.

Huntington, Sidney, as told to Jim Rearden. 1993. *Shadows on the Koyukuk: An Alaskan Native's Life Along the River*. Seattle: Alaska Northwest Books.

Langdon, Steve J. 1993. *The Native People of Alaska*. Anchorage: Greatland Graphics.

Merrill, Yvonne Y. 1994. *Hands on Alaska: Art Activities for All Ages*. Anchorage: K/ITS.

Morgan, Lael. 1979. *Alaska's Native People*. Vol. 16, No. 3. Anchorage: Alaska Geographic Society.

Murphy, Claire Rudolf, and Charles Mason. 1994. *A Child's Alaska*. Seattle: Alaska Northwest Books.

Paul, Frances Lackey, and Rie Muñoz. 1996. *Kahtahah: A Tlingit Girl*. Seattle: Alaska Northwest Books.

Renner, Michelle, and Christine Cox. 1995. *The Girl Who Swam with the Fish: An Athabascan Legend*. Seattle: Alaska Northwest Books.

Ritter, Harry. 1993. *Alaska's History: The People, Land, and Events of the North Country*. Seattle: Alaska Northwest Books.

Stauffacher, Sue. 1992. *S'gana: The Black Whale*. Seattle: Alaska Northwest Books.

Tripp, Angela, ed. 1994. *Alaskan Native Cultures: Tlingit, Haida, Tsimshian*. Santa Barbara, Calif.: Albion Publishing Group.

Wallis, Velma. 1993. *Two Old Women: An Alaska Legend of Betrayal, Courage and Survival*. Seattle: Epicenter Press.

———— 1996. *Bird Girl and the Man Who Followed the Sun: An Athabaskan Indian Legend from Alaska*. Seattle: Epicenter Press.

Wilder, Edna. 1987. *Once Upon an Eskimo Time*. Seattle: Alaska Northwest Books.

Winslow, Barbara, and Teri Sloat. 1995. *Dance on a Sealskin*. Seattle: Alaska Northwest Books.

▶ *A whalebone arch towers above the Arctic Ocean shore in Barrow, where Eva Nageak plays under the Midnight Sun.*

Alaska Northwest Books®
An imprint of Graphic Arts Center
    Publishing Co.
P.O. Box 10306
Portland, OR 97296-0306
503-226-2402; www.gacpc.com

Printed in Hong Kong

Library of Congress Cataloging-in-Publication Data:
Brown, Tricia.
    Children of the midnight sun : young native voices of Alaska / text by Tricia
Brown ; photographs by Roy Corral ; foreword by Larry Merculieff.
        p.   cm.
    Includes bibliographical references.
    Summary : Photographs and text present the experiences and way of life of Tlingit,
Athabascan, Yup'ik, Aleut, and other Native American children in the villages, cities,
and bush areas of Alaska.
    ISBN 0-88240-500-4
    1. Indian children—Alaska—Juvenile literature. 2. Eskimo children—Alaska—
Juvenile literature. 3. Aleut children—Alaska—Juvenile literature [1. Eskimos—
Alaska.]   I. Corral, Roy. 1946- ill. II. Title
E78.A3B76   1998
979.8'004971—dc21   97-41534   CIP   AC

Originating Editor: Marlene Blessing; Managing Editor: Ellen Wheat;
Editor: Linda Gunnarson; Designer: Elizabeth Watson; Map: Gray Mouse Graphics